COCKER SPANIELS

KATIE LAJINESS

Big Buddy Books
An Imprint of Abdo Publishing
abdopublishing.com

BIG BUDDY DOGS

abdopublishing.com

Published by Abdo Publishing, a division of ABDO, PO Box 398166, Minneapolis, Minnesota 55439.
Copyright © 2018 by Abdo Consulting Group, Inc. International copyrights reserved in all countries.
No part of this book may be reproduced in any form without written permission from the publisher.
Big Buddy Books™ is a trademark and logo of Abdo Publishing.

Printed in the United States of America, North Mankato, Minnesota.
092017
012018

THIS BOOK CONTAINS
RECYCLED MATERIALS

Cover Photo: Getty Images.
Interior Photos: AF archive/Alamy Stock Photo (p. 11); Drew Angerer/Getty Images (p. 5); Getty
    Images (p. 7, 9, 13, 15, 17, 19, 21, 23, 25, 27, 29, 30).

Coordinating Series Editor: Tamara L. Britton
Contributing Editor: Jill Roesler
Graphic Design: Jenny Christensen

Publisher's Cataloging-in-Publication Data

Names: Lajiness, Katie, author.
Title: Cocker spaniels / by Katie Lajiness.
Description: Minneapolis, Minnesota : Abdo Publishing, 2018. | Series: Big buddy dogs |
    Includes online resources and index.
Identifiers: LCCN 2017943927 | ISBN 9781532112072 (lib.bdg.) | ISBN 9781614799146 (ebook)
Subjects: LCSH: Cocker spaniels--Juvenile literature. | Dogs--Juvenile literature.
Classification: DDC 636.752--dc23
LC record available at https://lccn.loc.gov/2017943927

CONTENTS

A POPULAR BREED

Around the world, there are more than 400 dog **breeds.** Cocker spaniels belong to the Sporting Group. This breed is friendly and gentle. Let's learn why cocker spaniels are the twenty-ninth most popular breed in the United States!

Cocker spaniels have won Best in Show at the Westminster Kennel Club Dog Show four times!

THE DOG FAMILY

Dogs come in all shapes and sizes. Yet all dogs belong to the **Canidae** family. The name comes from the Latin word for dog, which is *canis*. This family includes coyotes, foxes, wolves, and more.

Humans and dogs have lived together for at least 16,000 years. In the beginning, humans **bred** them to hunt. Soon, they trained dogs to do other jobs such as guarding property and herding livestock.

Since 1935, the cocker spaniel has been one of the most popular dogs in America.

COCKER SPANIELS

More than 600 years ago, writer Geoffrey Chaucer wrote about a hunting dog called a *spaynel*.

This **breed** caught birds called woodcocks. Over time, the dogs earned the name cocker spaniel.

Today, the spaniel family is large. Some are water spaniels, and some are land spaniels.

A dog's sense of smell is up to 100,000 times stronger than a human's.

Over time, the cocker spaniel became an all-American **breed**. In 1878, it joined the **American Kennel Club (AKC)**. And, in the early 1960s, President Richard Nixon had a cocker spaniel named Checkers.

Did you know?

The AKC includes the cocker spaniel in the Sporting Group. Sporting dogs are excellent hunters.

Lady (*right*) from *Lady and the Tramp* is a cocker spaniel. The original movie came out in 1955.

WHAT THEY'RE LIKE

Cocker spaniels are gentle, happy, and smart. As a smaller dog, this **breed** has both speed and strength.

They are known to be friendly to strangers. And, they live well with other pets.

The grooves on the bottom of a cocker spaniel's paws inspired a shoe design. Paul A. Sperry made the Top-Sider with grooves on the bottom to prevent slipping on wet boat docks.

COAT AND COLOR

A cocker spaniel's coat is soft and thick. Its fur can grow very long. And, it can be straight or wavy.

Cockers can have black, brown, red, or cream coats. Some have white fur with patches of other colors.

14

Many people have their cockers groomed in the same style. The hair on the back is cut short. The hair on the sides, legs, and ears is longer.

SIZE

Cocker spaniels are small dogs. They stand about 15 inches (38 cm) tall at the shoulder. The males weigh about 25 to 30 pounds (11 to 14 kg). The females are somewhat smaller.

The **breed** has short legs and a deep chest. It has a rounded head, long ears, and big, brown eyes. And cockers usually have **docked** tails.

Cocker spaniels are the smallest breed in the Sporting Group.

FEEDING

All dogs need food and water to supply energy. Quality dog food provides important **nutrients**. Dogs can eat moist, semimoist, and dry foods. Puppies eat three or more small meals a day. Adult dogs eat one to two times a day.

Controlling a dog's daily food intake helps keep it at a healthy weight.

CARE

Dogs require a lot of care. Cocker spaniels need brushing to keep their coats healthy. These dogs need to visit a groomer to help keep their coats free of tangles. A groomer will also bathe the dogs and trim their nails. A dog should have its nails trimmed once a month.

Did you know?

Cocker spaniels should often have their ears checked. The long ears should be cleaned weekly.

Brushing helps owners check a dog's coat for skin problems and bugs.

Even the healthiest cocker spaniels will have some health problems. So, they need to visit a veterinarian regularly. The vet can provide health exams and **vaccines**. He or she can also **spay** or **neuter** the dog.

Puppies will need to see the vet several times during the first few months. Adult dogs should visit the vet once a year for a checkup.

By age three, 80 percent of dogs will have gum disease. Regularly brushing a dog's teeth will help its mouth stay clean.

Every dog needs a collar with identification tags. A **microchip** can also keep a dog safe. This way, an owner can find the pet if it gets lost.

At home, a crate offers a cocker a place to rest. It can also help with housebreaking puppies.

As hunting dogs, cocker spaniels want to run free and explore. That is why they need a leash when on walks.

PUPPIES

A cocker spaniel mother is **pregnant** for about 63 days. Then, she gives birth to a **litter** of five or six puppies.

They are born blind and deaf. Two weeks later, they can see and hear. At three weeks, the puppies take their first steps.

Did you know?

A newborn cocker spaniel weighs as much as two lemons.

26

In a few weeks, puppies' senses begin working and their tails start to wag.

THINGS THEY NEED

At eight to 12 weeks old, cocker spaniel puppies are ready for **adoption**. When a puppy comes home, the owner should begin obedience training as soon as it is settled.

Cocker spaniel puppies like to be active. So, they need daily exercise and training. This **breed** will be a loving friend for 13 to 15 years.

28

Every year, 5 million puppies are born in the United States.

GLOSSARY

adoption the process of taking responsibility for a pet.

American Kennel Club (AKC) an organization that studies and promotes interest in purebred dogs.

breed a group of animals sharing the same appearance and features. To breed is to produce animals by mating.

Canidae (KAN-uh-dee) the scientific Latin name for the dog family. Members of this family are called canids. They include wolves, jackals, foxes, coyotes, and domestic dogs.

dock to cut short, especially a tail or ears.

litter all of the puppies born at one time to a mother dog.

microchip an electronic circuit placed under an animal's skin. A microchip contains identifying information that can be read by a scanner.

neuter (NOO-tuhr) to remove a male animal's reproductive glands.

nutrient (NOO-tree-uhnt) something found in food that living beings take in to live and grow.

pregnant having one or more babies growing within the body.

spay to remove a female animal's reproductive organs.

vaccine (vak-SEEN) a shot given to prevent illness or disease.

ONLINE RESOURCES

Booklinks
NONFICTION NETWORK
FREE! ONLINE NONFICTION RESOURCES

To learn more about cocker spaniels, visit **abdobooklinks.com**. These links are routinely monitored and updated to provide the most current information available.

INDEX